Praise for
Nick McCormick's first book,

*Lead Well and Prosper: 15 Successful Strategies for Becoming a Good Manager*

"*Lead Well and Prosper* is a powerful little book that can reap huge rewards in your personal and professional life. I especially enjoyed Nick's action plans!"
-- Pat Croce, entrepreneur, motivational speaker, and
*New York Times* best selling author

"Don't read *Lead Well and Prosper* unless you want to be a great leader."
-- Phil Martelli, head coach, Saint Joseph's University
Basketball, author of *Don't Call Me Coach: A Lesson Plan for Life*

"*Lead Well and Prosper* is a wonderful book for managers. It is logical, clear and to the point. It describes the rules of management, and shows what should and should not be done in order to lead well."
-- Rhonda Dibachi, former executive vice president, Niku, Inc.,
co-author of *Just Add Management*

"The title says it all! Nick's 15 strategies are the fundamental building blocks that any manager can use to build a prosperous career."
-- Rob Waite, author of *The Lost Art of General Management*

"Simple, straightforward message that will help any manager reach higher."
-- Bob Prosen, best selling author of *Kiss Theory Good Bye*

"This book provides an important reminder on how to conduct yourself in a way that will make you and your team better. Most good leaders, whether they be coaches, players, managers, or CEOs, learn to master their own behavior first, before they try to lead others. This book is a quick and entertaining read that will reinforce the importance of building the right leadership habits into your daily life."
-- Fran Dunphy, head coach, Temple University Men's Basketball

# ACTING UP
## Brings Everyone
# DOWN

**The Impacts of Childish Behavior
in the Workplace**

By

## Nick McCormick
Illustrated By Mark Morgan

Be good PUBLISHING

Downingtown, Pennsylvania

First printing 2010
ISBN: 0977981347
ISBN-13: 9780977981342
Library of Congress Control Number: 2009914248

ATTENTION CORPORATIONS, UNIVERSITIES, COLLEGES, AND PROFESSIONAL ORGANIZATIONS: Quantity discounts are available on bulk purchases of this book for educational, gift purposes, or as premiums for increasing magazine subscriptions or renewals. Special books or book excerpts can also be created to fit specific needs. For information, please contact Be Good Publishing, 102 Patrick Henry Drive, Downingtown, PA, 19335; 610-518-2126.

# Acknowledgements

Thanks to the many who have helped me the past couple of years. I have learned quite a bit and have benefited significantly from your assistance.

Thanks to my wife and children for their patience and support as I continue to pursue my *Good Ventures*.

# Table of Contents

# Introduction

ALTHOUGH MOST OF US OVER the age of twenty-one look like adults, we don't always act that way. This author included! Going to work seems to bring out the kid in us—and I don't mean that in a good way.

Some would argue that we're treated like kids at work, and that's why we act like kids. There is probably some truth to that. Managers deservedly get beaten up about treating workers like children. I've been a manager most of my working career and I'm guilty of doing it myself. We do have a choice though—to rise above the childish treatment from management and act like adults...like adults should act that is!

There is something to be said for acting like a kid. Unfortunately, we tend to lose the positive traits of children—the wide-eyed wonderment, imagination, and playfulness—but we keep the less than favorable traits of entitlement, selfishness, whining, arguing, and so on.

I wrote a book a couple of years ago to help managers improve called *Lead Well and Prosper*. This book is much more inclusive. It's for everyone, including managers. After all, managers act like children too. In fact, they are some of the worst offenders.

The purpose of this book is to point out the silliness that we engage in at work in hopes that readers will acknowledge their actions, realize there are better and more constructive ways to act, and make the necessary changes to improve the work environment. There is so much to be gained by doing so.

This is by no means an unabridged anthology of childish behavior at work. I'm sure after reading the book you'll be able to come up with countless additional examples on your own. If you do have some that you'd like to share, please drop me a note on my website, www.BeGoodVentures.com. I'll keep them in mind for the next edition.

The fictitious characters that played such a large role in *Lead Well and Prosper* have returned to assist us with this book. Joe Kerr (a.k.a. Joker) is the veteran manager who "knows it all." Wanda B. Goode is the more junior employee, always looking to improve. They and their coworkers and friends will help bring the examples of workplace dynamics to life.

## Chapter I

# The Dog Ate My Homework

**Don** (Joe's boss): Joe, where's that report I asked for last week?
**Joe**: What report?

**Don:** The inventory report that you said you'd have for me yesterday.

**Joe:** Oh, right...that one. I didn't get to that, Don. I've just really been swamped with client requests this past week. Do you still need it?

**Don:** Yes, I still need it.

**Joe:** I'll drop everything and get to it right away.

We certainly do make a lot of excuses. The dog ate my homework is the classic excuse used by kids. Yup. Fido swallowed that assignment whole—certainly wasn't my fault. Sure, I buttered it and put it in his doggy dish, but who would have thought he'd actually eat it?

In general, kids aren't willing to fess up to wrong-doing.

**Mom:** Who did that?

**Wanda and Joey (simultaneously):** Joey/Wanda did it.

Then when they get caught up in a lie, they get emotional. I guess they figure it might get them off the hook. Or, maybe they just see their case starting to crumble. Maybe it's a bit of both. In any event, when facts fail to convince, kids give emotion a shot.

*Joey:* (fighting back tears) Don't you believe me, Mom? You don't believe me, do you? You always liked Wanda better than me!

Lots of adults aren't very good at fessing up either; at least there is much evidence that they struggle with it while at work. Other groups are blamed. Vendors are blamed. Equipment is blamed. Software is blamed. Rarely does someone (especially a manager) come out and say, "It was my fault. I blew it." It takes a bit of courage to do so. We could use a bit more courage in the workplace.

When adults are challenged, their reaction is defensive and emotional too. We whine, we get angry, we deny, we make excuses. I've heard some great excuses over the years. Here are some tried and true ones often invoked with the aim of shirking responsibility.

Some play dumb. "Oh, I didn't realize you still wanted that report (never mind that it's been due every week for the past two years). If you still want it, sure I'll get it to you." In other words, it's not my fault, but yours. You did nothing to convince me that you still needed it.

Some keep it simple when they neglect to complete a task and just say they were too busy. "Got tied up." Usually they throw in the "I was serving the customer" line. "You don't want me to ignore the customer do you?" Or, "I was working on the other project. I thought that was more important."

If all else fails, "I forgot" is a classic fallback. It worked at age five, so why not at age thirty-five? "I promise that I won't let it happen again (or at least until the next time you remember to follow up)."

Kids typically aren't very responsible. They have mom and dad to fall back on. At work, we have our boss or the company to fall back on. In matrixed organizations, no one really knows who's responsible for anything. Some embrace this flaw and take full advantage of it, spending a good deal of time trying to avoid or redirect blame.

Have you ever witnessed what happens when a group of adults is responsible for making coffee in the break room, or God forbid, cleaning the break room? It's a recipe for disaster. It makes you want to cut your kid some slack for missing the toilet and neglecting to clean it up—a minor mishap when compared to what results when "adults" are asked to clean up after themselves.

There's nothing like a good snow storm to heighten our irresponsibility. As kids, we'll stay up half the night watching the snow, hoping school will be closed the next day (at least that's what I did). Some adults do the same thing. After all, snow gives us a built in excuse. "Boy that traffic was brutal, Boss. I almost turned around a couple of times. I'm just glad I stuck it out. I'm lucky I got in by noon."

If we embraced our responsibility, upon hearing of an impending snow storm, we'd hit the hay early and then get up early in order to shovel and make it to work on time. Instead, we'll wake up later—"I'm sure it will take people a while to get in; might as well get some more shut eye." Next day, it's up and at 'em at 9:00AM. "Boss, the main roads were fine, but I couldn't get off my street. For some reason, they just haven't gotten around to plowing it yet."

Ever notice how kids will do almost anything rather than pick up after themselves, like cleaning their rooms. They actually work much harder to avoid what they don't want to do, than it would take to just do the task. They'd rather argue for twenty minutes than take five minutes to get the job done.

This phenomenon is common in the office environment as well. The fact that employees are being asked to do more and more allows them plenty of items/tasks to substitute for those they don't like to do. For instance, no matter how busy, the average worker always seems to have time for non-work related activity. A 2005 web survey by America Online and Salary.com found that American workers "fritter away" 2.09 hours/day not including lunch.[1] Surfing the Internet was cited as the number one time-wasting activity. At a time where people are "busier than ever," they have time to check the scores of the game last night or download some music from iTunes. Why? Because, checking the Internet is more fun and it's given a higher priority; and why not "stick it to the boss since she now has me doing two jobs?"

---

[1]    Research conducted through AOL's Find a Job site on AOL.com. Survey involved more that 10,044 respondents. Americans Waste More Than 2 Hours A Day At Work, www.salary.com

My point is not to address the Internet abuse problem. Rather, it is to show that people always have time for what they want to do. It applies to the busiest of busy people. Much like kids (and quite a few adults for that matter) are drawn to picking their noses, employees are drawn like magnets to certain unproductive tasks. No matter how frequently they are told, "Don't do it," they can't seem to help themselves. Tasks they are supposed to do will not get completed as a result.

What is a worker to do? Distractions are so numerous, and self-discipline is so low. There is no silver bullet. The key is to recognize when it's happening. Once there is awareness, there is a fighting chance to rise above the childishness, take some responsibility for our actions and inactions, and make the choice to get the job done. We must invoke our will and dare to be different!

---

**Do**

- Take responsibility. Yes, you are an adult. You can and should do it.
- Fess up when you screw up. It's an admirable quality. You will be respected more for doing so.
- Knock out those boring, pain-in-the-butt tasks first, so you don't have to make up excuses for not doing them. Then go surf the net.

**Don't**
- Make excuses—solve problems instead.
- Pick your nose!

## Chapter 2

# I'm Leaving and Taking My Ball with Me

*Joe:* I need Sam back on the Donleavy project.

> **Wanda:** Joe, there are only two weeks left on the project. If you yank Sam now three months of effort may go up in smoke.
>
> **Joe (thinks):** What do I care? When I first offered up Sam, I was supposed to get credit for some revenue from the project. Don says that's not going to happen now, so if I can't play, the game is over!
>
> **Joe:** I'm really sorry, Wanda, but I need Sam now.

How annoying was this when you were a kid? You probably did it yourself. "I'm leaving and taking my ball with me." I remember one particular kid when I was growing up used to sing it. The translation for the catchy tune was quite obvious, "If I can't have fun, no one else can." Why? Because if they have fun without me, they won't need me anymore. They'll just need my ball. Well guess what, my ball and I are a packaged deal, so you people need me to have fun.

Similarly, ever notice how a kid won't play with a toy for a year, and then as soon as another kid picks it up, it's the hottest toy around and no one else is allowed to touch it. Someone else likes the toy, so all of a sudden it has value.

This scene plays out at work all the time, especially among managers. If they see no benefit to themselves for a particular initiative, they won't participate. Or, if they are involved and the benefit dries up, they pull up stakes. They'll take their resources (their balls) and go home.

How about when the boss wants to give someone else responsibility for an area that has been neglected? Suddenly, the treadmill in the brain starts spinning a bit. "That's my turf. Sure I haven't done anything with it in over a year other than complain about it, but it is mine. I want that area. I love that area. I'll do anything in my power to keep that area. No one can have it but me (Because if I lose it, what's next? They'll move me right on out the door!)."

What a difference it would make if we actually did things for the good of the organization and fellow co-workers instead of just ourselves...if we stopped trying to build empires, stomping out those that "get in our way," if we shared credit...if we shared anything!

Not surprisingly, much of the childish behavior exhibited by adults and explained in this book results from fear—fear of losing a job, fear of losing out on a promotion. We need to realize the best way to conquer the fear is to meet it head on. If there is fear about losing a job, start planning for the next one. Learn something new. Do some positive things rather than wallowing in the mud.

**Do**

- Let others play with your balls. (You know what I mean!)
- Put your interests aside for a higher cause.
- Address you fears with positive actions.

**Don't**

- Be a scrooge.
- Act like a jerk. (This is one of my favorite pieces of advice!)

# Chapter 3

# Liar, Liar, Pants on Fire

**Wanda:** Joe, did you get that bonus approved yet?

**Joe:** (crossing his fingers) Not yet, Wanda, but I'm glad you stopped by. I just wanted to let you

> *know that I've been working like a dog for you this week. I've really stuck my neck out this time. If I don't get it approved, it certainly will not be for a lack of effort.*
> **Wanda:** *I really appreciate that, Joe.*
> **Joe:** *That's what I'm here for, Wanda. I'm here to help.*

Kids, like their grown up parents, lie. Some lie like rugs. They do it to avoid embarrassment. They do it to avoid punishment. They do it to impress—to dupe others into thinking they're better, more important, more powerful, and so on. They do it because they don't want to stand out from the crowd; they're more interested in self-preservation. They do it to gain acceptance and praise. They do it to put others down, in hopes that it will raise them up.

Kids also make lots of promises, don't they?

> **Joey:** *Mom, I'll never miss my curfew again. I promise. I'll be home by eleven. Please let me go to Sam's house.*

If I had a nickel for every time my kids promised something and didn't deliver, I'd have an ample supply of nickels. If I had a nickel for every time an employee/co-worker promised something that went undelivered, I'd have many, many more nickels!

Adults get carried away, just like kids. Sometimes the lies are brazen." I did not have sexual relations with...that woman!" Sometimes they are a little more subtle. In still other cases, they don't start out as lies, but the results are quite similar.

We get caught up in the moment. "Sure, Boss, I can do that. I'll do that too...and that...and that." We continue to say, "Yes" because we want to please. We want to be liked. We want to show our value. We want to keep our jobs.

Then, inevitably, commitments are missed. What's the response? "I'm doing five things, what do you expect?" Resentment builds. "I'm working my butt off and this clown complains about a lousy due date."

Guess what? If you sign up for five things, you need to do all five of them well and on time. The efforts to please, show value, and the like are squandered when promises are broken. I'm not sure why so many promises are broken, but it probably has something to do with the fact that there is typically no penalty for not honoring commitments and there is no reward for honoring them. The bar has most certainly been lowered. Honoring commitments no longer seems to be an expectation of the job. It is now seen as being exceptional.

Making promises is like a game for most. They are made just to keep ourselves in it. Sure, we may have every intention of doing what we say, but we certainly don't worry about it if we can't pull it off. That's just the way it is.

Kids foolishly think they can meet commitments up until the second they are due. "Joe, you have less than half an hour to do your homework and mow the lawn. You're toast." "No way man, I can still get it done." For this reason and for fear of consequences, they rarely give mom and dad a heads-up about their predicament.

At work, people do the same thing. If they are late with a task, they don't inform the boss, or other stakeholders. They go along as if all is well.

If kids can't pull off a miracle when they're in over their heads, their next hope is that mom and dad forget. This scene also plays out constantly in the workplace. Employees take on too much and they don't ask for help until things fall to the floor, and someone actually notices.

There is an alternative. It's OK to say, "No more, Boss, I'm already doing X and Y. If I take on Z, I won't be able to do X or Y well or on time." In almost every case, your boss will understand. S/he will assign Z to someone else, or instruct you to stop work on X and/or Y in order to get Z done. In other words, allow for the opportunity to reprioritize.

Have you ever noticed how kids make commitment and then break them when they get a better offer?

Wednesday
*Ted:* Joey, want to come over my house on
    Friday?
*Joey:* Sure.

Thursday

***Sam***: *Joey, my dad got tickets to the ballgame on Friday. Want to come with us?*

***Joey***: *Sure.*

Friday

***Ted***: *Don't forget to bring your glove when you come over after school today, Joey.*

***Joey***: *Uh...listen, Ted. I'm not going to be able to make it today. Something suddenly came up.*

The same is done at work. Again, managers are great at this because they have so many meetings and, thus, so many opportunities for conflict. They are ecstatic when a client meeting is scheduled at the same time as an employee review or some other potentially confrontational meeting. "Sorry, got a client meeting. We'll need to reschedule." This can be extremely damaging, especially if a manager stomps on the time of an employee. It sends the message, "You are not that important." Not good.

**Do**

- Your job well and tell it like it is. We could use some more honesty in the workplace.
- Honor your commitments, even if something better comes along later.
- Give stakeholders a heads up if you think you may be late with a task. Reprioritization may help get you back on track.

**Don't**

- Lie—it makes you look foolish.
- Bite off more than you can chew. That gigantizoid five-scoop ice cream sundae sure looks tempting, but the last scoop or two are tough to get down.

# Chapter 4

# Mom, Joey Hit Me!

*Joe:* Why did you get a chocolate cake for Bruce's birthday? You know I don't like chocolate.

*Wanda:* Bruce happens to like chocolate, and so does everyone else in the office. If you have such a problem with my choice of cakes, why don't you get the next one?

*Joe:* You know I don't have time for that. You're just trying to annoy me.

Kids bicker and quarrel. It's what they do. They fight over the most ridiculous things.

"Mom, Joey touched me!"
"Mom, Joey looked at me funny!"
"Mom, Joey called me a loser!"
"Mom, Joey won't let me play with him!"

You wouldn't think this type of behavior would occur in the workplace, but anyone who has worked in an office environment knows that it does.

There are those that openly quarrel with peers and management alike. Most will act like pre-teens and go off and whine among peers, occasionally going to management (i.e., mom or dad) with their complaints.

"Joe smells."
"Mary talks too loud."
"Joe comes in too late."
"Mary gets special treatment."
"Joe is a brown-noser."
"Wanda keeps information to herself."
"Mary is out to get me."
"Did you hear what Joe did the other day?"

I could go on and on, and I'm sure you could too. Unfortunately, whining doesn't accomplish anything. It's much better to focus on what you are supposed to do and not worry so much about others. If you are having a problem with someone in the office and you just can't let it go, try addressing it directly with the person. "Joe, when you do X, it really makes me feel Y. I probably shouldn't feel that way, but I do. Could you please do me a favor and stop doing X?" Nine out of ten times that will do the trick. In most cases, the "offending party" will be grateful that you brought it up and will accommodate your wishes.

Talking and complaining behind people's backs is counterproductive. It poisons organizations. If you are deathly afraid of bringing the issue to the attention of the "offending party," or if you have and it hasn't worked, go to your manager and ask that it be addressed. Make sure you follow up. Don't let your manager off the hook until it's resolved.

*Cliques*

Cliques are common with even the youngest of children. The "cool" kids have a way of ganging up on, and dressing down the "un-cool." Kids make fun of one another. They call each other names. They hold grudges. They pick favorites, and try to get their favorites to join them in their ridicule of others. I suppose it's mainly done to lift them up. It usually doesn't work out that way though. Of course, that doesn't seem to stop them from trying.

Yes, cliques do indeed thrive in the workplace. Groups of workers beat down others for working too hard, or for not doing things the "way we always do them." Sometimes it's overt. Sometimes it's not. It's never a good idea to talk behind someone's back. It doesn't matter if it's a superior or a subordinate. If a colleague gives you some dirt on another person, aren't you left wondering what the person says about you when you're not around?

My advice for those in the cliques: Break free and make some new friends. You too should aspire to stick out like a sore thumb. There are too many people going through the motions and following others like lemmings.

Speaking of lemmings, we've all heard this before. We may have even said it to our own children.

**Mom:** Joey, Why did you do that?
**Joey:** Sally was doing it.
**Mom:** If Sally were to jump off a bridge, would you do that too?

Kids do what other kids do. They wear what other kids wear. Once an item becomes "popular," all the kids just have to have it. Fads get created very quickly. My daughter went to a make-over birthday party. The eight-year-old girls could pick from four different kinds of hair extensions. They all chose the same one.

Adults at work operate the same way, especially managers. Most are followers. The higher up the manager, the more this seems to be the case, as ego is inserted into the equation.

> ***Joe** (**thinks**): Both Charlie and Bob had the new blackberry at the board meeting. They must know something that I don't. Plus, I can't let them show me up.*
>
> ***Joe**: Betty, get me the new Blackberry, and make sure it's loaded properly with my schedule.*
>
> ***Betty**: Right away, Sir.*

Whether it's purchasing a toy, or implementing the latest quality initiative, managers have to do what the others are doing. They don't want to be left behind. They also want to have a rock solid alibi should things go astray. "They call Bob a genius and he used supplier X. If Bob got it wrong, how can I be accused of making a bad decision?"

It is the extremely rare manager/executive that swims against the tide. It's too risky. Sure, some brag about how they disregard conventional wisdom, when in fact they don't. They talk about how they are contrarians when it suits them, but they really don't do anything differently. In fact, if you hear someone bragging about going against the tide, chances are very good they aren't.

*Bullying*

Some kids are just plain bullies, aren't they? They pick on others for the fun of it. Many bosses fit into this criterion. Some co-workers do as well. Sometimes, like children, workers raise their voices to attempt to intimidate. It works occasionally. "My oh my, I really must have upset Joe. He's carrying on like I challenged his manhood (or ate his lunch). I better not challenge one of his ideas again."

If you are a bully, work on your inadequacies, and while you are doing so, refrain from taking them out on others. Try building a person up. It's a lot more fun and rewarding. Although it takes much more time and a lot of effort to build a snowman than it does to knock one down, the building process is more fun. It lasts longer, and it's a lot more rewarding. For the victims, call the bullies to the carpet when necessary. Don't take them too seriously.

*Pettiness*

Adults can be extremely petty. Again, the egos...

"Mary tried to show me up. I'll show her."
"Joe shot down my idea. Let's see what happens the next time he asks me for a favor."

"Joe hasn't worked a day in his life. I've seen more initiative in a boulder, and at least a boulder doesn't snore."

"Mary went to my manager to complain about me. She'll never see another raise from me."

"I'll just leave out that critical piece of information so Joe fails."

We need to rise above our pettiness and do what is best for the organization. Rarely do our efforts to subvert others pay off in the end.

---

**Do** 👍

- Block out the noise. It takes two to tango. If you do have an issue with a co-worker, it's usually best to confront the person— not combatively. "Wanda, when you do X, it really makes me uncomfortable..."

- Build people up.

- What's necessary for the success of the organization?

- Leave your ego out of the equation.

- Make up your own mind. Sure, you can and should seek input/counsel when appropriate, but don't just do something because someone else is doing it.

- Look to take advantage of lemming mentality. If everyone is doing something one way, it may be a wonderful opportunity to do the opposite.

---

- Worry so much about others—focus on your job instead.

- Whine and bring down other workers with you—instead, confront the problems and offer up solutions.

- Be a bully. It's one of the most pathetic, lowly characteristics. There's no place for it in the playground or the workplace.

- Be so petty.

- Play favorites.

- Talk about others behind their backs.

- Be a Lemming. As your mother would say, "God gave you a brain, so use it!"

**Don't**

# Chapter 5

# Try it. You'll Like It

**Wanda:** Tom, how would you like to take on this new project. It's a little bit of a stretch, but I think you can pull it off.

**Tom:** I don't think so, Wanda. I'm really kind of busy right now. I don't know how I'll fit it in.

**Wanda:** I'll put Sam on that ABC project to free you up.

**Tom:** Oh, I can't abandon my project like that. Stick Sam on this new one. I'll get the next one, Wanda. I promise.

Some kids are adventurous. Many others are not. The latter seem to have a very special skill. They know what foods they like without tasting them and what games they like without playing them. I'm not confident that this skill is 100 percent accurate. It's quite possible they are missing out, don't you think?

Similarly, many adults don't like to try new things. They avoid change at all costs. They will go to extraordinary means to keep things exactly the way they are. They will employ the entire box of kid tricks in order to do so (e.g., lying, feigning cooperation, taking their ball home with them, etc.).

We all know it's important to grow. Most strive for job security and this is one of the few ways we can help ourselves in that department. Let's stop acting like timid toddlers and start acting like those fearless little maniacs. Let's get dirty and try something new. We need to experience the joy of breaking through our discomfort and grow, grow, grow.

Sometimes we are so ingrained in a process that we can't imagine it being done any differently. This is when some fresh blood is required to shake things up a bit. Welcome the new comer(s). Realize that "This is the way we've always done it" isn't a reason for doing something a certain way. Be open to the new comers' ideas. Learn from them, and try to make their ideas work.

Kids are great procrastinators. They'll put things off until the bitter end. It drives us adults crazy when they do it. "Joey, if you had just started studying a week ago instead of tonight at 8:00 PM, you wouldn't be in this situation." Yet, we do the exact same thing. We don't start on the project until the last minute. We'll read our mail, clean our desks, get a cup of coffee— anything to delay. We don't try to learn new things until we've lost our job. Then, guess what? It's too late. Procrastination is a form of self-sabotage and a built in excuse. "If I don't do so well, it's because I didn't have time to prepare." It can be devastating. I honestly believe that the difference between success and mediocrity lies in the discipline to move toward our goals prior to there being a crisis. Anyone can react to a crisis, but it takes a special person to act every day and actually avoid the crisis altogether.

Kids do (or don't do) many things that end up hurting them. They can be very stubborn. I'll show him. I just won't go to his birthday party. Result: Kid misses party, is completely miserable, and nothing gets resolved.

How many times do we do the same at work? "Are they kidding? They expect me to go to that training on my own time so I can make more money for them? Screw them! I'm not going. I'll just say I was sick." Result: Instead of learning a skill and becoming more valuable within and outside the company, the person languishes in a state of limbo, increases his/her bitterness toward the company, and lessens management's view of him/her. Talk about shooting oneself in the foot.

---

**Do** 👍

- Get dirty (you know what I mean), and try something new. Start small, and consistently execute.

- Welcome the newcomers into the organization. Encourage them to challenge existing rules and processes. Learn from them. Help them change the status quo.

---

**Don't** 🚫

- Sit like a bump on a log and let everything pass you by, and then complain that you don't get your way.

- Shoot yourself in the foot. Don't let anyone or anything get in the way of your own self-improvement—take advantage of opportunities for training and guidance offered by your company.

Chapter 6

# Gimme, Gimme, Gimme!

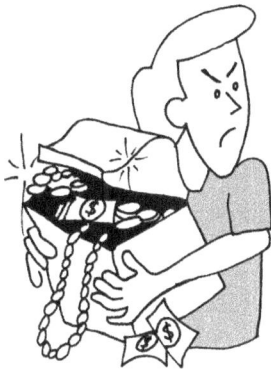

*Joe:* Can you believe they put me up in this cheesy hotel? They don't even have room service.

***Wanda:*** *Didn't you say you stayed at that same hotel with your family on your last vacation?*
***Joe:*** *Sure, but that was a vacation. This is business. Are you telling me we can't afford it? All these other schleps at the conference are staying at the "Lap of Luxury Hotel," and here I am at the "Room for a Few." I'll show them. I'm going to spend every cent of that meal allowance.*

Kids are selfish. They don't have much self-control. They want what they want, when they want it, and they want it now. They crave immediate gratification. Try telling a child to put something off today for something better tomorrow. It's nearly impossible. Recently my five-year-old son came into my room babbling incoherently. His cheeks were swollen and a rainbow of colors dripped from his mouth. It didn't take long to figure out that he had gotten hold of the gumball machine refill container. He stuffed so many gumballs in his mouth that he couldn't even speak. I had to rush him to the bathroom and have him spit out the gumballs before he choked to death. Why would he do such a thing? First, he loves the little sugar balls. They taste great, and more is better, right? Second, he didn't want anyone else to have them. He wanted to have them all to himself.

I know a lot of adults that react similarly. The credit card debt in the U.S. is testament to that. And how about all of the corporate and political scandals? People want what they want now, and some will do whatever it takes (even if it's not legal) to get it.

Kids have an intense feeling of entitlement too. They need and deserve to have everything they desire from the biggest piece of pie to the latest video console. They aren't exactly great stewards of their possessions either. If they neglect or mistreat something and it breaks, a replacement magically appears. It's not their money, so who cares?

In the working world, adults react similarly. They need to have the largest salaries, the latest and greatest equipment. They want a new computer every year, yet the one they have at home is seven years old. There is no concern for what something costs, whether the business is making money or losing money, whether it will go bankrupt or not. The concern is for them in the here and now. After all, they have credit cards to pay!

They run expense reports up like drunken sailors. They use office supplies to stock their homes. What's the justification? Usually there is some rationalization. "The company has loads of money. They won't miss a few pens." They've been mistreated in some way, shape, or form. They haven't gotten what they deserve, so they'll get theirs some other way.

Most people simply don't understand business. A business needs to make money. Global competition has intensified over the last few years, and businesses are under more pressure now than ever. The typical worker is oblivious. Managers don't help the cause by hiding and hoarding information. They also don't help when they announce cuts to the workers, but continue to spend wildly themselves..

> ***Worker:*** *We can't have any more offshoring of jobs. We need to keep wages high.*
>
> ***Enlightened One:*** *Who will pay for the high wages?*
>
> ***Worker:*** *What do you mean, who will pay? Just stop the offshoring. My salary isn't keeping pace with inflation. I have bills to pay.*
>
> ***Enlightened One:*** *Well guess what, the product we sold last year for $50 now sells for $25. Our costs are too high and you can't get a raise. You're lucky your salary hasn't been cut. Who will we sell our products to at twice the market rate?*
>
> ***Worker:*** *How is that my problem? That's for the big wigs to figure out...the government too.*

Employees react similarly when their ideas requiring investment are not embraced.

> ***Worker:*** *Corporate is so cheap. Why don't they just invest the two hundred thousand in this idea of mine? It will be worth two million in another year or two."*

My question back to these people is, "Are you confident enough in this idea of yours that you'd borrow from your 401K to make it happen? Let's pretend this is your money. Would you replace the ten thousand dollar printer to gain that extra productivity, or would you deal with the one you have for a bit longer?"

Now I'm not saying that all companies treat their employees wonderfully, maximizing the money they spend on them, and that they are all exceptional stewards of the corporate coffers. I am saying that frequently, there are two sides to the story and we need to be open to both. But first, we need to understand both.

Employees need to understand that the 50 percent profit on product/service X is not net money. Companies pay for healthcare. They pay for overhead items and taxes take a chunk out of the gross profit figure as well. Employees do understand that they only got a 2 percent increase, but that's only part of the story.

So how do we fix this one? The rank and file need to be educated. It's the job of those that do understand the business to explain it to those that don't. There's no reason to hide information here. The more knowledge that people have, and the more that things are out in the open, the better. Disclose as much as you can. Show the people where all the money is going. Show them how your competitors are getting things done.

When kids don't get what they want, they cry. Boy do they cry. Adults on the job do the same thing. "I can't believe we don't get free doughnuts at our meetings anymore. Those cheap bastards!" Some spend large portions of their day whining. They long for the good old days. In addition to the whining, kids usually let you know that something is not fair.

> *Joey:* Mom, it's not fair; Sammy has a Wii and his dad lets him stay out until 12:00.

Funny thing is that we don't really concern ourselves with fairness until we think we're being treated unfairly. If others are being treated unfairly, well that's their problem. "The rules seem quite fine to me!"

What it's really about is "What's in it for me?" Just as kids lobby for additional allowance for doing chores, we do the same at work. We want to know the benefit to us before we do something. When incentives are placed before us, we quickly determine the best way to meet them (regardless of the value to the company) and we set about doing them.

When kids don't get their way, some throw up their hands in defeat. Others don't give up so easily. One of their favorite ploys is to keep asking the same question until they get the answer that they like. They will frequently play one parent against the other.

At work, some will ask until they get an affirmative. They naturally go to the person that has the best odds of giving them a yes. If that doesn't work, they move on.

Much like children act as if their parents were born yesterday, workers act the same way toward their bosses. Although the actions of some bosses validate this belief, the odds are very good that the stunts the workers pull have been pulled by the very people they are pulling them on. The current generation has not invented the concept of acting like a child at work. Their forefathers have blazed a trail that has since become well worn.

---

**Do** 👍

- Be grateful for what you have. If you think you're worth more, prove it. Make your case and present it. If you are unsuccessful, it may be time to move on.
- Be a steward with the company coffers.
- Take some time to ask someone at work about the financials behind the business of your company. The next time someone complains about salary or money not being spent, pass your newfound knowledge along.

---

**Don't**

- Act like a selfish brat.
- Use company resources recklessly.

---

## Chapter 7

# Give 'Em an Inch,
# They'll Take a Mile!

*Joe:* They said a collared shirt was OK. This is a
collared shirt isn't it?

**Wanda:** Yes, but it isn't exactly appropriate for the workplace. Why don't you at least button up a bit, Joe?

**Joe:** I didn't see anything in the rules about buttons. Listen, this is the way I dress at home. Am I supposed to buy all new clothes just to participate in dress down day?

From the time they are a mere year or two old, kids are already testing their parents.

"Just 5 more minutes Dad."
"Mommy is sh@t a bad word?"

They will also stage open rebellions.

"I'm not going!"

Similarly, adults are constantly testing their bosses.

They test work hours like kids test curfews. They test the dress code like kids test the dress code. They test what happens when commitments are missed. They test out-of-office time ("I'm not feeling so good"), like kids test absences.

"I thought you were OK with me taking a day off, Boss. Last year you gave me an extra sick day, so I didn't think it was such a big deal."

How about the way kids will just stop doing things as soon as you stop nagging them? Joey's been told to make his bed every morning, and he's been doing so for years. He tests by skipping the chore one morning. Mom doesn't notice. Joe stops making his bed.

**Mom:** Joe, why haven't you made your bed?
**Joey:** I thought I didn't have to any more.
**Mom:** Why not?
**Joey:** You didn't say anything when I missed Monday.

This scenario translates easily to the workplace with any recurring deliverables, especially with things like status reports. "You didn't ask for it last month. I assumed you didn't need it any more!"

You are a grown up. Yes, some rules are silly. Make an effort to change some of them (by offering up alternatives) if possible. Don't just blurt out how stupid something is. That typically puts others on the defensive (typically those that created the rules!), and it gets you labeled unfavorably. And don't just stop doing something without letting someone else know of your intention.

Sometimes it's best to just bite the bullet with the trivialities. Sure they are irksome, but don't let them consume you. And don't just weasel out of doing them.

**Do**
- Grow up! You want to be treated like adults—start acting the part!

**Don't**
- Stop doing something just because someone doesn't reprimand you—ask permission first.
- Test your boss by stretching the rules— check first to see if it's OK. There are instances where it will make sense to break a rule, and that's fine. Don't hide it, just explain it.

# Chapter 8

# The Sky is Falling

*Joe:* If we don't get that quote to the client by tomorrow, we'll lose the business. The budget will be shot.

*Wanda:* You really think so? They just asked for it yesterday.

*Joe:* Listen, they are moving fast. If we can't show that we can keep up, they certainly

> *won't value us as a vendor. I need some help on this now. If I don't get it, these guys will walk, and we won't meet our numbers.*

Kids like to exaggerate. It helps them get their way.

*Joey:* Mom, if I don't get that book I'm going to fail my test. You don't want me to fail do you?

As kids, we learned and honed the skills. At work, we continue to master the craft of exaggeration. "If we don't get that software by Friday, the project will fail." "If I don't get that quote to the client by tomorrow, we'll lose the business." "If we down-staff by a person, the department will collapse."

The reason we do this is we feel we won't get any action unless we make the ramifications of inaction appear like an emergency. We have management to thank for this. The squeaky wheel approach to management is alive and well. We are a very reactive species, and we typically choose inaction when faced with a difficult choice. Exaggeration is not the answer though. Rather, spending more time honing your pitch and explaining the impact/ value your suggestion will have on the decision maker and the organization is more appropriate, and frequently more effective.

We also exaggerate our value. Many of us spend half our time on the job working to convince others how difficult our job is.

The simple fact is, everyone is replaceable. Everyone! So, don't even bother wasting your time on that nonsense. Rather, spend it on acquiring new knowledge and skills. Make yourself more valuable within and outside of your company.

No one wants to get laid off. We all want to keep our jobs. We like to eat. We like to have a roof over our heads. We know there is no such thing as job security. The best we can do is improve our employability. We don't do that by protecting our territory to ensure that we are the only person on the team that can input entries into the proprietary general ledger system. There is not much value in that. What is the market outside of our organization for that skill set?

When we over-exaggerate our importance, it is only a matter of time before the truth is revealed. Then we look like a cad, and we're screwed. We find that we're not prepared to do anything else, because we spent all of our time feigning our importance rather than learning new skills.

---

**Do** • Learn. Learn. Learn. Improve your value by learning new things. Train someone else to learn what you already know so you can go off and do something bigger and better.

---

• Exaggerate. You won't get taken seriously once the jig is up; spend your time honing your pitch and selling the value/impact of your idea to the decision-maker.

Don't

• Worry excessively about being replaced—don't spend time trying to convince others of your value. Rather, channel that energy and fear into learning something new.

## Chapter 9

# Can't We Just Glue It?

*Joe:* I'm a tad behind on my project.
*Wanda:* Do you think you can get back on track?

*Joe:* If management forks over a little more cash, we have a shot. We need more people.

*Wanda:* I've heard the project is already running over budget. Are you sure throwing more money at it will work?

*Joe:* Of course it will. Besides, we don't really have any other options.

Kids have a way of oversimplifying things. For example, they become familiar with the properties of such things as glue—that it bonds things together. They've seen it in action. It fixes things. They then assume that glue is the fix for everything, from a shattered window, to a malfunctioning TV, to a broken heart.

*Janie:* Can't we just glue, it?

*Mom:* No, Janie, we can't.

*Janie:* Well why not? How about if we super glue it?

*Mom:* Glue won't fix this problem. Glue can't fix everything.

Managers are experts at over-simplification. They typically have good intentions, but they rarely take into account the ramifications of their decisions. They frequently mix up the relationship between cause and effect. For instance,

"Sales have been down in the past few years. In the good old days, five years ago, when things were hopping the sales team was wearing suits. Now they are not. We need the sales team to start wearing suits again. That will get us back on track."

It's this type of backward thinking that contributes to the preponderance of office satire. There is no thought as to whether wearing suits had anything to do with prior sales success. Further, there is no thought to the ramifications of the decision. Do clients want to see sales people in suits if they themselves are not similarly suited? Will it make them uncomfortable? Does the sales force even have suits, or will they have to acquire a whole new wardrobe?

We love to oversimplify: Kids think their parents have an endless supply of money.

*Mom:* I don't have enough money to buy that, Joey.

*Joey:* Go to the machine and get some more.

*Mom:* Joey, it's not that simple. We don't have any money in the bank.

*Joey (thinks):* The bank always has money. That's why it's called a bank. Why can't we just get more money out of the bank?

Simple, right? Just get some more money. I don't care how you get it. Just get it so I can get my toy.

We discussed this in Chapter 6, "Gimme, Gimme, Gimme." We do the same thing at work. Sales are down. The market won't allow an increase in price. The company is losing market share to competitors, but Joe wants his increase.

*Joe:* I need my increase. I have bills to pay. Have you seen the gas prices?

*Boss:* Joe, there's no money to give. Sales are down. Profits are down. We're getting beaten up by global competition. We're lucky we have jobs at all. We may not in a few months if we don't find a way to do things better.

*Joe:* Don't tell me we don't have more money up at corporate. Who is paying for that corporate jet?

Have you ever seen a young child play hide-and-go-seek? They do at least two very interesting things. One is, they cover their eyes, and because they can't see you, they assume that you can't see them. The other thing they do is hide in the same spot over and over and over again. It's as if the prior game (that they enjoyed so thoroughly) never took place.

At work, we frequently put the blinders on. We ignore the realities. We frown on potential improvements. We tend to do what we know. If it worked before, we repeat it, regardless of the circumstances. We make the same mistakes over and over again. Sometimes we expect different results, but most of the time, we're just very comfortable with the mistakes. They are familiar. We know how to fix them. They become part of the process and a reason for our existence.

Managers appear to own many pairs of blinders. They get much use. Managers will continue to make decisions without involving the staff. When I got my teeth cleaned recently, the hygienist told me I was sitting in a brand new chair. The dentist had ordered the chair, which cost several thousand dollars without telling her. Turns out when it first arrived, she couldn't use it. Instead of coming with a foot pedal to raise the position of the chair, it had a hand control, similar to a computer mouse. She explained that since hygienists typically work alone, they can't keep removing their gloves to reach over and reposition the chair. That's why the foot pedal is so convenient. She ended up taking her concern to the dentist and he ordered her a foot pedal. Of course, this could have been avoided if the dentist got input on her requirements first. In addition to getting the order correct, it would have given the hygienist more sense of ownership. This is a simple example, but similar things occur over and over again in the workplace.

Managers continue to avoid addressing problems until they blow up. They continue to make the same silly mistakes—revenue dips a bit, cuts are made to customer service, revenue dips more due to poor customer service, more cuts are made, revenue dips more. The cycle continues until the product/service is wiped out. Then they repeat the same thing over and over again.

It happens in all areas of business. How many times have you seen retail chains go on a building spree? Buildings start popping up all over the place—one thousand stores this year, two thousand the next, and so on. The market inevitably gets saturated and the stores begin to close. The addiction to growth is the blinder. No one can see past that, despite the fact that it has occurred over and over again.

---

**Do** 👍

- Challenge your old assumptions. Experience is a good thing, but what worked yesterday on one type of problem won't necessarily work on the same or similar type of problem.

- Before making a decision, carefully assess the impact to other stakeholders. Get input from others. Examine the ramifications.

- Be conscious of the blinders we sometimes wear. Invite others into the decision making process. Be open to alternatives. Your way is not always the best way.

---

- Issue unilateral decisions without input from those impacted and no thought to how to deal with exceptions.

**Don't**

- Assume that what worked in the past will work in the future.

- Assume your way or the highway.

- Assume.

# Chapter 10

# Isn't That What You Asked For?

*Joe:* No one leaves until this production run is finished.

*Next Day*

*Joe:* What's going on here? You weren't supposed to leave until the run was finished.

*Bill:* It did finish.

*Joe:* But 50 percent of the product is defective!!!

*Bill:* You didn't say anything about defects. You
asked that the production run be finished.
Isn't that what you asked for?

A similar scenario plays out between children and their
parents all the time.

*Dad:* I thought I asked you to cut the lawn.

*Joey:* I did cut the lawn.

*Dad:* You didn't do the trimming.

*Joey:* You didn't ask me to trim. You asked me to
cut the lawn. Isn't that what you asked for?

If kids don't want to do something, they will take off their
thinking caps and do exactly what you ask, nothing more, nothing
less. OK, I'll admit it; sometimes they'll even do less! Sometimes
you can ask children a couple of questions and they'll only answer
the one they want to answer. Sometimes they won't answer any
of them at all.

Employees are no different. If they want to get back at the
boss or the company, they will do the same. They don't think

much about the ramifications to them if their behavior impacts their boss or company.

My brother had a screen door installed. He came home from work to find the installer wrapping up the job. Unfortunately, the door did not fit. It was a couple inches too narrow for the door opening. After pointing out this obvious problem, the worker responded, "This was the door they gave me to install, so I installed it. If you have a problem with it, you'll need to take it up with the shop," and off he went.

This form of passive resistant behavior is common when there is conflict between departments, between categories of workers, and between management and worker bees. It's incredibly childish, and it goes on constantly, sapping productivity and making workers miserable.

Rise above this behavior. As a child, this wise cracking, rebellious passive resistance may have been great for irritating mom, dad, and others in position of authority, but your employer typically doesn't love you unconditionally like mom and dad. It won't do you any good in the workplace.

---

**Do** 👍 • Rise above the petty "I'll show him" behavior. Do your job and do it well. Take pride in a job well done.

---

• Poison the work environment with passive resistant behavior. Even if you don't plan to stay at your current job, never burn a bridge. It's a small world, and it's getting smaller every day. You never know when a screw up will come back to haunt you.

Don't

# Chapter 11

# I Can't Hear You

*Wanda:* I think I found a way to cut the time it takes to create this report in half.

*Joe (thinks):* I've got to get out to the web this afternoon to book that trip to Barbados.

*Wanda:* I've been playing around with some Excel macros...

*Joe (thinks):* I can't wait to hit those beaches.
*Joe:* That's great, Wanda. Hey listen, I need to get going. I need to make a phone call.

How many of you have seen kids make some sort of noise, cover their ears and pretend that they can't hear you? "AHHHHHHH. I can't hear you. AHHHHHHH. I can't hear you. AHHHHHHH." When kids don't want to hear what you have to say, they make it painfully obvious. "Talk to the Hand!"

Believe it or not, I have witnessed people do the same exact thing at work. It's usually done with a bit of humor, but the message is clear. More often, we display our disinterest by cutting people off or by not paying attention. We read email, answer phone calls, and other such things. This gives the person on the other end a crystal clear message. You don't want to hear it.

I don't know about you, but I hate going to the doctor's office. The interminable waiting and being shuttled around like steer until the doctor is ready is dehumanizing. My biggest gripe, though, is that most doctors don't listen.

Once placed in the examining room, after a few more minutes of waiting, a nurse typically arrives. I provide a detailed explanation of my condition to the inquiring nurse, who scribbles some notes. I'm not sure why, because the doctor apparently doesn't consult with the nurse or read the notes.

Upon arrival, an additional ten to fifteen minutes later, the doctor appears to have no idea what the problem is, as I'm asked to repeat everything I just said to the nurse. Unless I have things written down, it's rare that I get through what I've come to say, because the doctor has already cut me off and decided the method of treatment, which inevitably requires the drawing of blood. Before I know it, I'm out of there. I waited an hour to see the doctor for two minutes.

Whether in a doctor's office, in a PTA meeting, or in the office, it's not a good feeling when your audience doesn't listen to you. You don't want people to feel like they do after an appointment at the doctor's, do you?

We need to unload our hang-ups. We don't listen to those younger than us, because we're more experienced and obviously know better. We don't listen to those older than us, because they are just old farts and time has passed them by.

Bill Russell, winner of eleven NBA championships (two as a player/coach) is credited with the following quote: "If you don't listen, you can't win." We need to listen to what others have to say. We need to hear criticism and openly address it as necessary. We need to be open to better ways of doing things. One of the best ways to learn is to listen to others. One of the best ways to improve is to listen to others. We don't have all of the answers. We need the help of others.

The first step is to ask. I'm amazed at how we do things that impact others without even bothering to ask for their input.

Remember the hygienist example? Asking followed by listening is incredibly empowering.

We can't succeed by listening selectively. People don't bother sharing with those that don't want to listen. This hurts the negligent listener along with the team and the organization. Lots of managers won't listen at all to any employee ideas. Then a problem arises that they can't address themselves and they put out the request for assistance. No one responds. Why not? They know the manager is just self-serving. Because the plea for assistance has gone unanswered, this affirms the manager's belief that there is no reason to listen.

---

**Do** 👍
- Ask for help. Ask people's opinions.
- Listen. Listen actively. Give people your undivided attention. You will be amazed at what you learn. You will be amazed at how engaged your organization will be.
- Get over yourself. Others do have a lot to teach you. Listen and you will learn.

---

**Don't** 🚫
- Dehumanize people by not listening to them.

---

# Chapter 12

# Now What?

**Wanda:** When will you have your task done, Joe? I need you to finish your part before I start mine.

*Joe:* I have no idea, Wanda. If things quiet down a bit today, I'll be able to work on it, but it's just been nonstop.

*Wanda:* Will you have it done by the end of the month?

*Joe:* Don't know. Best I can say is I'll be done when I'm done, and not a moment sooner.

Kids are very reactive. They don't typically do a lot of planning. They really shouldn't have to. They are kids, right? At some point, though, they need to start to learn to plan if they are to succeed in school and beyond. Some of us have a tough time learning this lesson.

As young children, it's the parents that dictate the schedules of their children. The parents tell the kids what to do.

*Mom:* Wanda, band practice is in half an hour; it's time to get ready to go.

*Wanda:* What should I wear?

*Mom:* Wear whatever you'd like.

*Wanda:* I need your help.

*Mom:* I'll be up in a minute.

The job of the kids is to show up.

*Wanda:* I'm here. Where are we going next?

**Mom:** *You have a party at Mary's after that. You'll have twenty minutes to change in between. I brought some clothes. You can change in the bathroom after practice.*

For some of us, this does not change once we become gainfully employed. We allow others to set our schedules. A ping on our computer tells us where to go. Then we show up. If we're managers, we typically show up late! We don't give much thought to what will be done during the meeting. There is no preparation. We just wait until someone starts talking and go from there.

Our mobile phone rings, we react to that. Our email pings, we react to that. We bounce from one meeting to the next, one task to the next, one distraction to the next, with no rhyme or reason, no prioritization of any kind. Then we look up at the clock and it's time to go home. "What a busy day," we pronounce. Then we start all over again the next day. The end of the week comes and the project that would have taken about an hour of uninterrupted time to complete is not finished. It was started twice, but it was not finished. "I didn't have time…too busy…" is the mantra.

It's impossible to be efficient when we just blow in the wind like this. A small amount of time taken to plan out the week's activity, a commitment to adhering to the schedule, and developing the ability to occasionally say, "No," will markedly improve productivity. Not only that, it will thrill others, because things will actually get done.

Some people will tell you they must answer their cell phone every time it rings. They must remain glued to their monitor to respond to their email just in case a message comes in. "Why?" is my next question. "Because people expect that I respond quickly." What happens when you leave the office at 3:00 because you are not feeling well? Are you still able to respond in 10 seconds to emails that come in? "Well no," is the response. Does the world stop turning as a result? "Well, not exactly." Then you can turn off the Blackberry for an hour to complete the assignment that you said you'd have completed by today.

Unless you are in an occupation where an immediate response is required (like a call center rep, or a heart transplant surgeon), you don't need to respond that quickly. The fact that you are trying to be so responsive, keeps you from responding to the things that matter. Most people are quite content with a response within a twenty-four hour period. How many times have you made a call to some sort of service provider and never gotten a call back? Is it comforting to know that the service provider can't get to your call because he/she is glued to the computer monitor constantly being interrupted by other first time calls?

I'm very passionate about the role that planning can play in improving the productivity of all workers. I included an appendix in my previous book describing the approach that I use and have included it in the appendix of this book as well (Appendix A).

It's very difficult to get people to change their approach to how they do their work. It's a very personal thing, and as a manager by day, I don't force my approach on anyone. I really don't think that one size fits all. The approach that works for me is an adaptation of many others, to include Stephen Covey. I encourage you to adapt and adjust it until you find something that works for you that you can call your own.

The bottom line though is that for it to work well, you'll have to have some sort of prioritization mechanism coupled with the ability to spend uninterrupted time on the most important tasks.

---

**Do** 👍

- Plan your week.
- Limit interruptions. You don't have to answer your mobile phone every time it rings.
- Turn off the ping on your email inbox.
- Restrict the amount of times that you read email each day.
- Check out the appendix for some additional tips on how to plan your week.
- Prepare for meetings.

---

**Don't** 🚫

- Get sucked into the world of fake urgency.
- Break commitments.

---

# Chapter 13

# I Won!

**Wanda:** Joe, I could really use some help on this project. I think Al would be perfect. Could I borrow him for about three months?

**Joe:** I really don't think I can do that, Wanda. We have a really tough couple of months coming up and Al is critical to our success. (He also happens to be our best hoops player and the playoffs are next month!)

Kids like to win, and they'll do just about anything to secure a victory. One common tactic is stacking the teams. "Joe, how can you say that the teams are fair? You have all of the best players?"

If you are a manager, have you ever stacked the teams? Have you hoarded the best people, keeping them from growing, so that you look good and get your way?

Kids make up their own rules too, don't they?

**Sammy:** *You're it!*

**Joey:** *No I'm not, I'm on base.*

**Sammy:** *What do you mean you're on base? We never even said bases were allowed.*

**Joey:** *Yes we did, and I'm on base! Nannannabooboo!*

Did you ever have a manager make up the rules or change them on the fly?

**Joe:** *We get this account and we'll all get bonuses.*

*(A few weeks later the account is secured.)*

**Wanda:** *Joe, when do we get our bonuses?*

**Joe:** *Turns out the account is not as profitable as we thought. There's no bonus money for that.*

Kids will flat out cheat too. Winning is so important to them.

*Sammy:* You just landed on my property.
*Joey:* No I didn't. I landed on Chance.
*Sammy:* Joey, you rolled a three.
*Joey:* I know I did. One-two-three.
*Sammy:* Joey, you were on Tennessee Avenue.
*Joey:* No I wasn't.

I don't want to go into a long dissertation about adults cheating on the job, but anytime there is something at stake, look out! Managers sandbag with budget numbers, employees pad their yearly accomplishments, people steal one another's ideas and call them their own, and the list goes on.

Even when kids lose, they will claim they won! They'll argue for hours unless parents intervene.

*Joey:* We won again. That's three in a row for the good guys!
*Sammy:* You didn't win. We did!
*Joey:* Are you nuts? You guys cheated and we still won!
*Sammy:* No way. We won that game!

Almost everything is made into a contest. Getting that coveted first spot in line is a huge win. "Me first!" I occasionally commute to work on a train. Adults battle to be the first ones off the train. The train is still moving, yet they get up and gather their things and walk down the aisle. They open the door ignoring the sign that says, "Don't open while train is moving." Why? Why do they do this? Will they get to work ten seconds faster? Will that make some sort of difference?

People just don't like to lose, and on the job it's no different. We don't even like to admit when we are wrong. Our egos are way too sensitive for that. It reminds me of something that my son used to say at the age of four, "Daddy, even when I'm wrong, I'm right!"

Winning is a lot of fun, and a little friendly competition is healthy, but winning at all costs is harmful. You may get the victory in the short term, but the long-term damage can be devastating.

**Do**
- Play Fair.

**Don't**
- Act like a jerk! (Told you I liked this one).

# Chapter 14

# Can't Means You Won't

***Wanda:*** *Joe, one of the guys just had a great idea. We could save time and reduce errors if we make a couple minor tweaks to our procedure.*

*Joe:* You're not advocating that we take short-cuts, are you, Wanda? You know we can't do that.

*Wanda:* It's not a short cut, Joe. It's an improvement.

*Joe:* Wanda, we've tried other "improvements" before. There is a reason this process has been around for twenty years. It works.

Have you ever gone shopping with a kid? They don't typically have much staying power. Apparently, after a few minutes their muscles atrophy to such a crippling state that they can't walk anymore. As a matter of fact, they can't even stand. They drop to the floor.

*Dad:* Get up off the floor, Joey, and come over here.

*Joey:* Daddy, I can't. I can't move.

Often, we give up too easily. We submit an idea. It gets shot down. We give up. We blame it on someone or something. It's usually not our fault.

Mom always used to say, "You can't means you won't." Resist the urge to say that you can't. Find a way that you can. This is actually the time to be relentless. Don't be content with trying. Rather, be content with succeeding. Rework your pitch. Make it better. Do it again.

**Do**
- Be open to new ideas.
- Persist.

**Don't**
- Give up.
- Get hung up on the way things used to be done.

# Conclusion

It's not illegal to take part in a lot of the childish actions described in this book. There are lots of things worse than acting like a child. However, the impacts of doing so are substantial. Funny thing is that we get annoyed at our children for pulling these stunts, and then we turn around and do them ourselves.

We are grown ups. It's time we start acting that way. Let's strive to drop the childish behavior and embrace the child-like behavior. Wouldn't it be great if we applied that child-like excitement to our job tasks? When was the last time you were so excited at work that you forgot to go to the bathroom?

Not that I'm advocating peeing in ones pants during work, but if it comes to that, I'll spring for the bodily fluid cleanup kit. Remember that stuff from school? Just sprinkle it on the offending fluid to harden it up and sweep it away.

Wouldn't it be wonderful if we had that problem? Imagine the productivity improvement? Offshore smoffshore!

It's in your power to make things better. Do it in spite of the boss. Do it in spite of the company. Life is too short to be miserable on the job and to allow that misery to affect our personal lives any further.

Be Good!

# Appendix A: Planning Your Week

Identify tasks/objectives to be completed — As they are scheduled in your calendar, mark tasks with an S (for "scheduled"). If there is no room in your schedule to complete certain tasks, mark them with an N (for "not scheduled") so they can be revisited the following week. Scheduling is complete when all tasks are marked with an S or an N. A sample task list and schedule follow.

- S Prepare for client meeting
- S Work on presentation for next week
- S Set up interviews next week for John's annual review feedback
- S Review training material
- S Work client issues
- S Work action items from last managers meeting
- S Complete monthly financial outlook
- N Work on proposal for XYZ company

## Sample Schedule

| | Monday | Tuesday | Wednesday | Thursday | Friday |
|---|---|---|---|---|---|
| 8:00 | | | | | |
| | Weekly planning* | Read email* | Read email* | Read email* | Read email* |
| 9:00 | Read email* | | | Weekly staff meeting * | |
| | Time reporting* | | Weekly project update conference call* | | One-on-one meeting* |
| 10:00 | Work client issues | Complete monthly financial outlook | | Publish mtng minutes* | |
| 11:00 | | | | Client meeting | Marketing conf call |
| 12:00 | | | | | |
| 1:00 | Set up interviews for John's review | | | Work on next week's presentation | |
| | | Monthly managers' meeting | | | |
| 2:00 | | | Prepare for client meeting | | |
| 3:00 | Work action items from last managers' meeting | | | | Expense reports* |
| | | | | | Purchasing approvals* |
| 4:00 | | Review training materials | | | |
| 5:00 | | | | | * Recurring items |

Here are some tips for making this work:

- Make sure you have all of your recurring meetings scheduled.
- Give yourself more time than you think you'll need.
- Don't schedule any meetings prior to 9:00 AM or after 5:00 PM. This will leave you extra time to get to unexpected items that will come up.
- If you finish up something early, pick off a future item.
- If you fall behind, see if you can make an adjustment to the schedule.
- Share the busy times on your calendar so people will schedule around you.

Before setting your schedule for the following week, review your performance from the prior week. Mark the completed items on your task list with an X. Think about why you didn't get the others done. Carry the unfinished items forward to your current week's task list and repeat the scheduling steps. Reward yourself when you have a good week.

# Appendix B: Do's

- Take responsibility. Yes, you are an adult. You can and should do it.
- Fess up when you screw up. It's an admirable quality. You will be respected more for doing so.
- Knock out those boring, pain-in-the-butt tasks first, so you don't have to make up excuses for not doing them. Then go surf the net.
- Let others play with your balls. (You know what I mean!)
- Put your interests aside for a higher cause.
- Address you fears with positive actions.
- Your job well and tell it like it is. We could use some more honesty in the workplace.
- Honor your commitments, even if something better comes along later.
- Give stakeholders a heads up if you think you may be late with a task. Reprioritization may help get you back on track.
- Block out the noise. It takes two to tango. If you do have an issue with a co-worker, it's usually best to confront the person—not combatively. "Wanda, when you do X, it really makes me uncomfortable..."

- Build people up.
- What's necessary for the success of the organization?
- Leave your ego out of the equation.
- Make up your own mind. Sure, you can and should seek input/counsel when appropriate, but don't just do something because someone else is doing it.
- Look to take advantage of lemming mentality. If everyone is doing something one way, it may be a wonderful opportunity to do the opposite.
- Get dirty (you know what I mean), and try something new. Start small, and consistently execute.
- Welcome the newcomers into the organization. Encourage them to challenge existing rules and processes. Learn from them. Help them change the status quo.
- Be grateful for what you have. If you think you're worth more, prove it. Make your case and present it. If you are unsuccessful, it may be time to move on.
- Be a steward with the company coffers.
- Take some time to ask someone at work about the financials behind the business of your company. The next time someone complains about salary or money not being spent, pass your newfound knowledge along.
- Grow up! You want to be treated like adults—start acting the part!
- Learn. Learn. Learn. Improve your value by learning new things. Train someone else to learn what you already

know so you can go off and do something bigger and better.

- Challenge your old assumptions. Experience is a good thing, but what worked yesterday on one type of problem won't necessarily work on the same or similar type of problem.

- Before making a decision, carefully assess the impact to other stakeholders. Get input from others. Examine the ramifications.

- Be conscious of the blinders we sometimes wear. Invite others into the decision making process. Be open to alternatives. Your way is not always the best way.

- Rise above the petty "I'll show him" behavior. Do your job and do it well. Take pride in a job well done.

- Ask for help. Ask people's opinions.

- Listen. Listen actively. Give people your undivided attention. You will be amazed at what you learn. You will be amazed at how engaged your organization will be.

- Get over yourself. Others do have a lot to teach you. Listen and you will learn.

- Plan your week.

- Limit interruptions. You don't have to answer your mobile phone every time it rings.

- Turn off the ping on your email inbox.

- Restrict the amount of times that you read email each day.

- Check out appendix A for some additional tips on how to plan your week.
- Prepare for meetings.
- Play Fair.
- Be open to new ideas.
- Persist.

# Appendix C: Don'ts

- Make excuses—solve problems instead.
- Pick your nose!
- Be a scrooge.
- Act like a jerk.
- Lie—it makes you look foolish.
- Bite off more than you can chew. That gigantizoid five-scoop ice cream sundae sure looks tempting, but the last scoop or two are tough to get down.
- Worry so much about others—focus on your job instead.
- Whine and bring down other workers with you—instead, confront the problems and offer up solutions.
- Be a bully. It's one of the most pathetic, lowly characteristics. There's no place for it in the playground or the workplace.
- Be so petty.
- Play favorites.
- Talk about others behind their backs.
- Be a Lemming. As your mother would say, "God gave you a brain, so use it!
- Sit like a bump on a log and let everything pass you by, and then complain that you don't get your way.

- Shoot yourself in the foot. Don't let anyone or anything get in the way of your own self-improvement—take advantage of opportunities for training and guidance offered by your company.
- Act like a selfish brat.
- Use company resources recklessly.
- Stop doing something just because someone doesn't reprimand you—ask permission first.
- Test your boss by stretching the rules—check first to see if it's OK. There are instances where it will make sense to break a rule, and that's fine. Don't hide it, just explain it.
- Exaggerate. You won't get taken seriously once the jig is up; spend your time honing your pitch and selling the value/impact of your idea to the decision-maker.
- Worry excessively about being replaced—don't spend time trying to convince others of your value. Rather, channel that energy and fear into learning something new.
- Issue unilateral decisions without input from those impacted and no thought to how to deal with exceptions.
- Assume that what worked in the past will work in the future.
- Assume your way or the highway.
- Assume.
- Poison the work environment with passive resistant behavior. Even if you don't plan to stay at your current job, never burn a bridge. It's a small world, and it's getting

smaller every day. You never know when a screw up will come back to haunt you.

- Dehumanize people by not listening to them.
- Get sucked into the world of fake urgency.
- Break commitments.
- Give up.
- Get hung up on the way things used to be done.

# Index

www.ingramcontent.com/pod-product-compliance
Lightning Source LLC
Chambersburg PA
CBHW060621200326
41521CB00007B/843